■ SCHOLASTIC

SUPER-FUN
MULTIPLICATION
MEMORY BOOSTERS

Kathleen Kelly & Stephanie Nunziata

New York • Toronto • London • Auckland • Sydney
Mexico City • New Delhi • Hong Kong • Buenos Aires

Teaching *Resources*

Kathleen would like to dedicate this book to her favorite thinkers: Hilary, Riley, Liam, and Finnigan. She would also like to acknowledge the Kelly family for their persistent support and her colleagues, particularly Stephanie, for their motivation and guidance.

∾

Stephanie would like to dedicate this book to her family, who has taught her how to live, to think, and to love life. She would also like to thank her colleague, Kat, who listens patiently and pushes everyone around her to make the world a better place.

Edited by Mela Ottaiano
Cover design by Scott Davis
Interior design by Solas
Interior illustrations by Doris Ettlinger

ISBN: 978-0-545-33281-1
Copyright © 2013 by Kathleen Kelly and Stephanie Nunziata
All rights reserved. Published by Scholastic Inc.
Printed in the U.S.A.

1 2 3 4 5 6 7 8 9 10   40   19 18 17 16 15 14 13

CONTENTS

INTRODUCTION

I tried to teach my child with books,

He gave me puzzled looks.

I tried to teach my child with words,

They passed him by, often unheard.

Despairingly I turned aside,

"How shall I teach this child?" I cried.

Into my hands he put the key,

"Come," he said, "and play with me."

~ Author unknown

How can we use the little time we have with our students in ways that maximize learning? As educators, we are constantly asking ourselves this question, trying to find the most efficient and meaningful ways to help our students learn. In this age of educational accountability, we must employ the most effective strategies to guide our students to optimal learning.

In this book, we have synthesized findings in the field of education regarding memory and applied them to create an effective approach to learning and recalling multiplication facts. Our approach is based on capturing the strength of the pre-multiplication skill of skip counting and then leveraging that skill into multiplication success. This approach enables students to move on to more complex mathematical tasks, with a strong arithmetic framework to support their thinking. It can be frustrating to work with a student on geometry or algebra concepts, only to be slowed down by his or her lack of retrieval speed and overall comfort level with basic math facts. We believe one of the contributing factors is little quality learning time spent on skip counting and multiplication facts, which produces math learners who, in the later years, are without confidence and unprepared for the rigor of higher-order math tasks.

Super-Fun Multiplication Memory Boosters will help you implement a comprehensive response to your students' learning needs in these basic math facts, particularly multiplication facts. You can use this memory-boosting approach with any math series, whether spiraled or linear, to augment students' higher-level skills by creating a solid base on which to build their understandings. The stronger students' competence in the basic facts, the more capable they will be at handling the increased complexity of higher math skills. For example, when we ask students to remember and implement the many steps of a long division problem, they need to have basic multiplication, division, addition, and subtraction facts at their fingertips before they can be successful at the higher level of thinking.

This book takes a multimodal approach to learning multiplication facts. Students work with a variety of tools in order to learn skip counting patterns as a foundation for fact retrieval. We call this "laying down the pathways." Then, students practice retrieving these facts by answering randomly generated multiplication questions. They first lay down the pathways with the movements and patterns and then deepen those pathways through high-interest interactions using manipulatives, movement, and healthy competition to generate problems and solutions. During the Fact Fluency Games, other students act as "checkers" so that there is instant feedback on the math facts. After all, it is not helpful for students to practice the wrong answers.

Goals of This Book

Super-Fun Multiplication Memory Boosters has six explicit goals:

1 Use neural science and kinesiology to reinforce neural networks dedicated to math fact retrieval.

2 Increase the speed and accuracy of math fact retrieval in all learners.

3 Create a comprehensive brain-friendly approach to math fact acquisition.

4 Generate positive attitudes to create a climate of success regarding math in general and math fact memory work specifically.

5 Provide simple, effective, accessible strategies for parents to use to help reinforce learning of math facts.

6 Create a robust web of activities to support learning and retrieval of math facts.

The Brain-Body Connection

Much recent research related to brain-friendly teaching has focused on the connection between the body and brain function. In fact, the importance of the brain-body connection is demonstrated in its inclusion as one of Geoffrey and Renata Caine's *12 Brain/Mind Learning Principles* (Caine & Caine, 2005). An understanding of the brain-body connection has helped educators evolve our approach to learning as we incorporate meaningful movement to aid in memory-making in our classrooms. In fact, Judy Willis, in her book *Research-Based Strategies to Ignite Student Learning*, shares, "in the classroom, the more ways the material to be learned is introduced to the brain and reviewed, the more dendritic pathways of access will be created" (page 4). This means that when we use different movements while teaching new information, it is more likely the students will be able to understand and retrieve this information later on. Learners will be able to remember more math facts if we engage the whole body in the learning process. In her treatise, *Smart Moves: Why Learning Is Not All in Your Head*, Carla Hannaford invites us to "understand the mind/body system's enormous innate capacity to learn and [recognize] the role of movement in activating that capacity" (page 14).

Developing Memory Pathways

There are two main aspects of memory: storage and retrieval. In order to have easy access to math facts, they must be organized and stored logically by a systematic approach to learning in the first place. It is imperative that patterns are utilized when trying to learn multiplication facts. After all, one of the main jobs of the brain is to seek patterns. We are reminded of this by Eric Jensen in his many publications focused on brain-friendly teaching. Our approach uses recent findings in the field of kinesiology to solidify the learning of the skip counting patterns as a precursor for memory work with multiplication facts. In *Learning With the Body in Mind*, Eric Jensen goes on to point out, "as learning institutions incorporate more physical activity and less lecture, all of our students, not just the kinesthetic learners or those lacking social skills, will experience increased intrinsic motivation, improved attitudes, more bonding and yes, even more brain cells" (page ix).

The Well-Traveled Path Allows an Easy Journey

Memory pathways are very similar to how paths are made in a forest. Imagine a forest you must pass through to get to a specific destination. You could take different paths through the forest to get to the destination. You would always arrive at the same place, but the journey would be different. Now imagine that you took the same path each time you went. That path would become well traveled: wider, with a deeper rut in it. This is how memory pathways work in your brain. If you use the same hook, or pathway, to arrive at multiplication facts, and practice often, that path will become well traveled and will provide quicker retrieval. Memory pathways become more permanent with use.

The more we ask students to retrieve "$4 \times 5 = 20$," the greater their fluency becomes in that retrieval. Since mathematical skills build on each other, it is imperative that the basics be well understood and amply practiced. What we require of students in upper grade mathematics calls for both speed and accuracy in math fact retrieval. While problem-solving strategies are a vital part of getting to answers for students, quick retrieval of math facts is an important part of success in intermediate and middle school math coursework.

Connections to the Common Core State Standards

As we embrace the tenets of the Common Core State Standards, we find confirmation of our belief that the "starter skills" of arithmetic—skip counting and fact fluency—are of utmost importance. What we know about the Common Core State Standards for Mathematics is that learners will increasingly need to rely on a very strong foundation of math-fact knowledge and recall in order to grapple with the elevated challenges presented by the new content standards. In a way, math instruction has been simplified to be more complex—what had become an overwhelming number of topics addressed each year has been whittled down, but each is being addressed in more complex ways. Problem solving that is focused on rigorous content and application of knowledge through higher-order skills is now at center stage. Certainly, strong competence in basic facts provides a fertile base for the more complex competencies that will challenge our young learners as they progress through the Common Core State Standards for Mathematics. Across the grade levels, the activities in this book will help you meet the following Standards for Mathematical Practice:

MP7: Look for and make use of structure.

MP8: Look for and express regularity in repeated reasoning.

Bibliography

Caine, Geoffrey & Renata. *12 Brain/ Mind Learning Principles.* Thousand Oaks, CA: Corwin Press. 2005

Hannaford, Carla. *Smart Moves: Why Learning Is Not All in Your Head.* Arlington, VA: Great Ocean Publishing, Inc. 1995.

Jensen, Eric P. *Learning With the Body in Mind.* San Diego, CA: The Brain Store, Inc. 2000.

Willis, Judy. *Learning to Love Math: Teaching Strategies That Change Students' Attitudes and Get Results.* Alexandria, VA: ASCD Publications. 2010.

Willis, Judy. *Research-Based Strategies to Ignite Student Learning: Insights From a Neurologist and a Classroom Teacher.* Alexandria, VA: ASCD Publications. 2006.

The Benefits of Movement

As we move to the practical aspects of our approach, it is important to know the "why" of incorporating movement with learning. Movement does many things for the learner. It can act as a stress reliever for a student who is not yet comfortable with mathematical tasks. In her book *Learning to Love Math: Teaching Strategies That Change Students' Attitudes and Get Results*, Judy Willis shares, "Before children can become interested in math, they have to be comfortable with it" (page 9). Moreover, the act of incorporating a specific movement with a specific number pattern, as in skip counting, ignites memory pathways in new and different ways that can positively impact learning. Movement and play can also act as a social bonding mechanism, which helps improve learners' self-concepts, which in turn can increase learning rates. So, with the "why" under our belts, let's turn to the "how" and get moving!

How to Get Learners Moving

Skip Counting Activities

Since skip counting can be a supportive tool for students who struggle with multiplication fact fluency, we begin by teaching students the skip counting patterns. We have matched a distinct movement with each number (2–12). Since another hook for effective memory is an emotional connection, we have connected meaningful stories and movements for each number. The activities are designed for students to enjoy so that they can develop positive feelings toward math in general and multiplication tables specifically. Experience tells us that enjoyment of math is key to success in math.

Fact Fluency Games

We use this collection of hands-on/minds-on activities to help students practice spontaneous math thinking. The idea that children must be competent at answering any basic math fact at any time before they can be competent as higher level math thinkers cannot be overstated. For example, in order to attain competence with long division, a child must have a firm grasp of addition, subtraction, and multiplication facts. The same goes for developing competency in geometry and algebra. These higher-level math thinking categories are predicated on a firm knowledge of the basics. If we allow our learners to proceed to these types of thinking without the required tools, we are setting them up to fail.

Game Materials: You can play these games using items you probably already have in your classroom, or you can create them easily from scratch. To get started gathering items you'll need, take a look at the Materials list on page 10.

Plastic storage bins with lids make great containers for all of the materials needed for each Fact Fluency Game. They not only help store the games when not in use, but also help make handing out the materials for each game an easy task. Use smaller, appropriately-sized containers for the manipulatives and keep them in the game bin. Students (and you) will find it easier to clean up and to keep things organized.

It's possible to use any dice you have around the classroom to play many of the games. However, incorporating a variety of dice brings novelty to a game and keeps it fresh.

For many of the games you can make the cards that go along with the game. (See individual Fact Fluency Games for more information.)

Try cutting 3″ × 5″ index cards in half to make them closer in size to typical playing cards.

We prefer not to use interlocking cubes so students can see the visual representation of multiplication as in three rows of four.

You do not have to use full-size soccer balls. Small colored versions can brighten up a game.

Materials

* beanbags (at least 2)

* butcher paper (approximately 4' × 4')

* construction paper (blue and red)

* dice
  traditional dice
  big blow-up dice
  foam dice
  dice-in-dice (a large clear outside die with a colored die inside)
  12-sided numbered dice

* dry-erase boards and markers

* bins or shoeboxes

* glue

* index cards
  multiplication flash cards (without products on the back)
  shape cards
  number cards
  product cards
  mystery number cards

* masking tape

* 1-inch blocks

* paper plates (13–26)

* permanent marker

* rubber mouse pads (15)

* soccer balls (3–5)

Optional
* buzzer; laminated array charts; addition, subtraction, and division flash cards; wet-erase (overhead) markers

Reproducible Resources

Skip Counting Posters: On pages 37–42, you will find a mini poster for each skip counting pattern (numbers 2–12). It is important for students to be able to match each movement with the skip counting pattern as well as be able to see the pattern visually. (See page 13 for more information.)

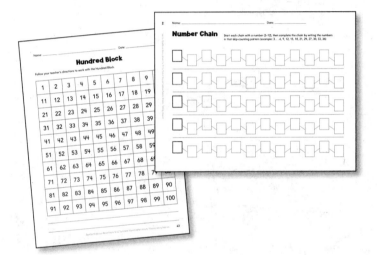

Skip Counting Reinforcement: On pages 43 and 44, you will find two activity pages for reinforcing the skip counting patterns students have learned. More detailed information on how to use the Hundred Block and Number Chain is on page 14.

Fact Fluency Games Student Directions:
It does not seem to matter how well you teach students a new routine or procedure, they always have questions! We have found it helpful to create bins for each game with all of the game's materials inside, including a laminated version of the student directions (pages 45–59). This way, students can review the directions independently while you are working with other students.

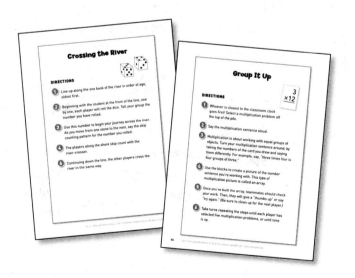

💡 Back the directions with construction paper before laminating.

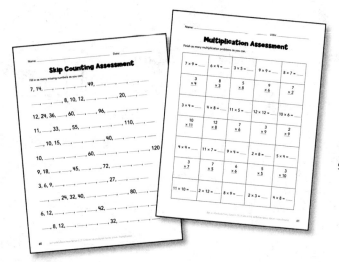

Assessment Sheets: These quick assessments (pages 60 and 61) will help you see how students are progressing in learning their skip counting patterns and multiplication facts. It is always a good idea to give one of these assessments as a pre-test, so you have a baseline of how much students know.

Parent Letters: It's important to get parents involved in supporting the important work your students are doing in school. Providing parents with fun ways to work with their child to reinforce basic computation facts can improve the automatic retrieval of random facts. We have included two samples of program-support letters to parents (pages 62 and 63) to model possible approaches you may take to invite parents into the learning process for your students. The sample letter on page 63 is geared to a second grade classroom, but can be adapted to fit your grade and students' needs. Whether you use these letters or create your own, be sure to communicate your teaching goals so parents know what to expect and how they can help.

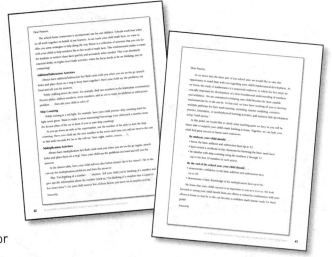

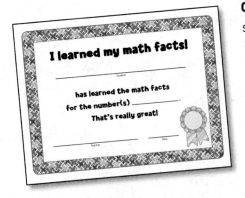

Certificate: We all love to be recognized. Celebrate with students as they learn new things. We use a certificate (such as the one on page 64) to celebrate when students have learned all the movements associated with skip counting, have mastered a difficult skip counting pattern, or have made a marked improvement in their math fact retrieval. When achievement is recognized publicly it spurs on students to learn new things and recognizes the hard work that went into their learning.

SKIP COUNTING ACTIVITIES

Skip Counting Basics

The following skip counting activities are a series of movements, designed to connect to the skip counting patterns for the numbers 2 through 12. Each number has a movement, and a story that goes along with that movement, to help it make sense for students. As we teach each of the skip counting patterns, our first expectation is that students learn the stories and movements that go with a given number. For example, before we expect students to learn 7, 14, 21, and so on, students need to know the Alligator move for the 7s pattern. We allow students ample opportunity to get these ingrained in their memories through repetition. Once children learn a movement, we add on the companion skip counting pattern.

While you are the expert in your classroom and know the path that makes the most sense for your students, we suggest teaching the movements in the following order:

* Start with the patterns that are more familiar to students, such as 2s, 5s, and 10s.
* Build from there with 3s, 4s, and 11s.
* Finish with the more challenging patterns: 6s, 7s, 8s, 9s, and 12s.

> We begin our skip counting movements with the 2s. Why?
> * There is no way to skip count by 0. It would simply go, "Zero, zero, zero . . ."
> * Skip counting by 1 is simply counting.
> It's helpful to include 0s and 1s facts, however, when you have students practice random multiplication facts.

As appropriate for your students' level, you may want to end the skip counting pattern with the eighth or tenth number. Keep in mind that the directions we have provided extend each pattern to its twelfth number.

Additionally, students find it helpful to have visual reminders of the patterns. Please see the Reproducible Resources section for mini posters (pages 37–42) you can photocopy and distribute to students. In our classrooms, we make large versions of the posters. Sometimes we use three colors to create a repetitive visual pattern for the numbers, which helps any student who needs that type of hook to remember the skip counting pattern. For example, you can highlight the first number in yellow, the second in blue, third in green, and begin the highlighting pattern again with the fourth number. You can make your own handmade large posters, or enlarge the reproducible versions by 200% to print on 11" × 17" paper or by 175% to print on 8 1/2" × 14" paper.

With practice, students will be able to perform the skip counting patterns with the movements in a variety of situations throughout the day. Once students learn the patterns, you can incorporate the movements anytime. For example, when lining up for lunch, direct students to "perform the sevens." This would have them doing their 7s movement (Alligators) while counting by sevens and walking toward the door.

When students demonstrate mastery of the first 12 numbers in each skip counting pattern for the digits 2–12, we call them "Skip Counting Experts." Once students have mastered these patterns, plan game centers so that they can have frequent practice at retrieving random multiplication facts in fun and engaging ways.

Skip Counting Reinforcement

Hundred Block: The following are suggestions about how to use the reproducible Hundred Block (page 43) for a variety of reinforcement activities.

* As you teach the different skip counting patterns, have students color in the squares involved. Encourage students to keep skip counting up to 100.

* Direct students to write about the pattern they see for each number they skip count by. For example, ask: *How does the pattern repeat itself? Is there a geometric shape created within the hundred block?*

* Students can build on the patterns by coloring different skip countings in different colors. For example, say: *First, skip count by 2. Color these squares yellow. Next, skip count by 4. Color these squares blue. Then, write a sentence about the pattern you see. Remember to think about how different numbers relate to each other.*

* Invite students to create riddles about numbers. Share this example: *My number is found when you skip count by 2 and by 3. It's bigger than 10 but smaller than 15.*

Number Chain: Number chains provide students an opportunity to look at skip counting in a different format. Often when we practice skip counting, the students are looking at posters of the numbers hanging vertically. When working with number chains, the students see skip counting horizontally.

Number chains provide practice for the automatic retrieval of the skip counting patterns. You can use them as "Do now" and "When you're done with your work" activities, as homework, or for assessment.

When you use the number chains in class, set a time limit. If students are working independently at a center, you can provide them with a small timer and allow them to set it themselves.

The following are suggested ways to use the reproducible Number Chain (page 44) effectively.

* Fill in the first square of each chain with the beginning number of the pattern. Have students complete the rest of the chain independently.

* Fill in three consecutive boxes somewhere along the chain and have the students figure out which skip counting pattern it is.

* Provide targeted homework by creating different number chains for different groups of students so each student is being challenged at an appropriate level.

2s: Windshield Wipers

The Story: "For the twos, we pretend our arms are windshield wipers on a car. As you 'wipe' across in front of your body, you think about the next number in the twos skip counting pattern."

The Movement: We use windshield wipers because it is an object that most children will recognize, but also because the movement crosses the body's midline (the imaginary line that divides your right side from your left), which is an important neurologic step for memory work.

1. Demonstrate the complete movement once before including the skip counting pattern.

2. Start with both arms bent at the elbows with your palms facing forward. Shift your arms to the left to begin the movement.

3. Wipe your arms from left to right, and then right to left.

4. Perform the movement again, this time with the numbers. Say "two" as you begin on the left side, then say each consecutive number just before you swipe your hands back the other way. Continue the movement until you have reached 24.

5. Have students try the movement. They should follow along with you to repeat steps 2–4.

3s: Karate Chops

The Story: "For our threes movement, we use karate chops. You can put up three fingers as you do the movement. This will remind your brain to focus on the threes while you do it! Imagine while you are performing the karate chops that you're chopping the air in front of you into thirds."

The Movement: Once again, crossing the midline of the body is an important part of this movement.

1. Demonstrate the complete movement once before including the skip counting pattern.

2. To start this movement, hold up three fingers on each hand.

3. Beginning with your right arm, chop that hand down diagonally from the elbow. Repeat with the other arm. (As you bring your left arm down, bring your right arm up, and vice versa.)

4. Perform the movement again, this time with the numbers. Say "three" as you bring your right hand down the first time. Continue the movement, switching arms and saying each consecutive number until you have reached 36.

5. Have students try the movement. They should follow along with you to repeat steps 2–4.

4s: Head Taps

The Story: "When we do our fours movement, we tap four fingers from both of our hands on top of our heads each time we say one of the numbers in the fours pattern. We are reminding our brain to count by fours on each tap."

The Movement: We want some of the movements, such as this one, to be simultaneous (right and left in concert) and others to be sequential (separating right movements from left). This offers physical novelty to the learners and helps differentiate one move from another.

1. Demonstrate the complete movement once before including the skip counting pattern.

2. To start this movement, place your arms comfortably in front of you and hold up four fingers on each hand. Then, raise both hands above your head.

3. Simultaneously, bring both hands downward and use the four outstretched fingers on each hand to tap your head.

4. Perform the movement again, this time with the numbers. Say "four" as you first tap your head with your fingers. Continue the movement, saying each consecutive number until you have reached 48.

5. Have students try the movement. They should follow along with you to repeat steps 2–4.

5s: Baseball Throws

The Story: "Baseball Throws for our fives patterns is one of my favorites because I like to imagine throwing a ball around. Fives are usually easy for us to remember, and this movement is a fun way to reinforce this pattern."

The Movement: Remember to have students cross their body's midline as they "throw."

1. Demonstrate the complete movement once before including the skip counting pattern.

2. Begin with your two fists in front of you. Your arms should be bent at the elbow with your fists at chest height.

3. Using your right hand, pretend you are throwing a baseball to someone who is to the left of you. Open your right hand as if you are actually releasing a ball. Point out that it looks like you're throwing your five fingers when you do it!

4. Repeat with your other hand.

5. Perform the movement again, this time with the numbers. Say "five" as you throw your first imaginary baseball. Continue the movement, alternating sides with each throw across your body and saying each consecutive number until you have reached 60.

6. Have students try the movement. They should follow along with you to repeat steps 2–5.

6s: Heel Lifts

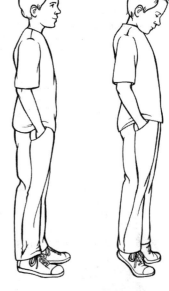

The Story: "For the sixes, we use our feet . . . that's something different! Sixes are one of those patterns that take a lot of time and practice to remember. So we perform this movement a little more slowly. Lifting our heels up takes us more time, which gives us more time to remember our sixes."

The Movement: It's important to involve the whole body. Using the feet in this movement is novel and helps keep the brain engaged.

1. Demonstrate the complete movement once before including the skip counting pattern.

2. Begin with your feet flat on the floor and about 6 inches apart. Then lift both feet up onto your toes.

3. Perform the movement again, this time with numbers. Say "six" as you lift up on your toes. Continue the movement. Each time you lift up on your toes, say the consecutive numbers in the pattern until you have reached 72.

4. Have students try the movement. They should follow along with you to repeat steps 2 and 3.

7s: Alligators

The Story: "The number seven looks a little like an alligator's mouth when it's wide open. Let's make the movements of an alligator's mouth as we 'chomp' our way through the sevens pattern."

The Movement: Kids love this movement—and connecting to that emotion is a great way to impact memory.

1. Demonstrate the complete movement once before including the skip counting pattern.

2. Turn your body sidewise to the right. Stretch your arms straight out in front of you with one arm on top of the other.

3. Move your arms wide open (one up, one down) and bring them back together, as if your arms are an alligator's mouth opening and closing.

4. Perform the movement again, this time with the numbers. Open your arms wide and as you close the alligator's mouth, say "seven." Continue the movement. Each time bring your arms together, say the consecutive numbers in the pattern until you have reached 84.

5. Have students try the movement. They should follow along with you to repeat steps 2–4.

8s: Star Pulls

The Story: "These are the opposite of the Baseball Throws we used for the fives. For the eights, instead of throwing your fingers away, you're pulling them in from the sky, like pulling down the stars!"

The Movement: Once again, focus on crossing the midline of the body in the movements and be deliberate as the children recite the number patterns.

1. Demonstrate the complete movement once before including the skip counting pattern.

2. Start with your left arm up diagonally above your head with fingers outstretched.

3. Pull down your arm crossing the midline. As you do this, close your hand into a loose fist as if you have just grabbed and pulled down a star. Repeat with the other arm.

4. Perform the movement again, this time with the numbers. Say "eight" as you pull your left arm down for the first time. Continue the movement, alternating sides with each pull and saying each consecutive number until you have reached 96.

5. Have students try the movement. They should follow along with you to repeat steps 2–4.

9s: Knee Lifts

The Story: "Knee lifts go with the nines because they both start with the /n/ sound! Knee lifts can take us a little longer to do, which is great, because learning to skip count by nines takes us a little longer!"

The Movement: Engaging upper and lower body parts *and* crossing the body's midline makes this a power move!

1. Demonstrate the complete movement once before including the skip counting pattern.

2. Start with your arms out to either side, at shoulder height, and bent at the elbow so that your fingers are pointing upward.

3. Alternate touching your right hand your left knee as you lift your left leg waist high, then touching your left hand to your right knee in the same way.

4. Perform the movement again, this time with the numbers. Say "nine" as you touch your right hand to your left knee for the first time. Continue the movement, alternating sides and saying each consecutive number until you have reached 108.

5. Have students try the movement. They should follow along with you to repeat steps 2–4.

10s: Headlights

The Story: "Headlights is a move that really only involves the fingers. When we learned the Baseball Throws, we threw one hand at a time. Since the tens are twice as many as the fives, we use both hands to 'flash' our skip counting for the tens."

The Movement: Students may be tempted to move more quickly on the simpler moves like this one. Help them understand that the brain needs time to focus on the pattern to learn it well and a slower tempo is best.

1. Demonstrate the complete movement once before including the skip counting pattern.

2. Begin by standing with both hands closed in a fist and held up at the sides of the body, bent at the elbow.

3. Open your hands at the same time and then close them, as if you were signaling flashing headlights.

4. Perform the movement again, this time with the numbers. Say "ten" as you open your hands for the first time. Continue the movement, saying each consecutive number until you have reached 120.

5. Have students try the movement. They should follow along with you to repeat steps 2–4.

11s: Lap Claps

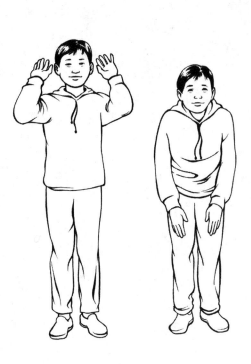

The Story: "What part of our bodies looks like the number eleven? Our legs, of course! So, this time we'll tap our legs as part of the movement."

The Movement: Visualizing engages important memory pathways. Legs make the perfect tool for learning 11s.

1. Demonstrate the complete movement once before including the skip counting pattern.

2. Starting with your hands up by your face, bring them straight down to lightly tap your thighs.

3. Perform the movement again, this time with the numbers. Say "eleven" as you tap your legs the first time. Continue the movement, saying each consecutive number until you have reached 132.

4. Have students try the movement. They should follow along with you to repeat steps 2 and 3.

12s: Shoulder Shrugs

The Story: "Of course, the twelves are the hardest pattern to remember. So the movement is one that we often use when we're saying 'I don't know.'"

The Movement: Tempo is important here, as the move is easily done, but the pattern takes a lot of focus to remember.

1. Demonstrate the complete movement once before including the skip counting pattern.

2. Put your arms out with your palms facing up and your elbows at your sides.

3. Shrug your shoulders up and then let them down.

4. Perform the movement again, this time with the numbers. Say "twelve" as you shrug your shoulders the first time. Continue the movement, saying each consecutive number until you have reached 144.

5. Have students try the movement. They should follow along with you to repeat steps 2–4.

FACT FLUENCY GAMES

The following games support students' practice of answering random math facts in a fun, motivating way so that the facts become more deeply ingrained in their thinking. The more we ask children to generate answers to arithmetic problems, the greater access they will have to that information. Repetition, particularly random repetition, fine tunes the "finder" in their brain that helps them locate the answers to the math facts that they already know and makes fact retrieval more efficient. Through these activities, students move from having to figure out the answers each time to accessing the prior learning from their memory banks. The more frequently we ask students to do this, the greater their success rates and the faster their pace of retrieval.

The games are sequenced from basic to complex. Each game requires a simple list of materials and comes with various amounts of support or challenge to provide you with options for adjusting the games to reach all learners and extend the learning.

We recommend dividing your class into three or four groups and using this smaller group size for playing each game. When introducing a game, do so as a whole-class activity, but use a small group of volunteers for the initial demonstration. Once students are familiar with the games, you can have multiple games going on at one time. The games are designed so that there is always something for each student to be doing. Sometimes students perform a skip counting movement on the side or act as checkers; sometimes the game is a team challenge.

> We have found that allowing students to learn many different games makes them feel like they are not just practicing multiplication over and over.

You will find the student directions on pages 45–59. Photocopy and laminate these sheets so students can refer to them as necessary. Simply distribute the directions and provide any necessary game materials so that students can work independently. You can work with small groups on other activities or travel from group to group to check on how students are doing.

The total amount of time you take to play these games is flexible. You may even choose to use them during center time; students can move to a new station whenever you typically have them rotate. The most important thing to remember is to change the games often so students are continually engaged. We also find that incorporating the activities on a regular basis is more important than devoting a large amount of time to them at once. You, of course, will best know the needs of your own students.

> Ultimately, the goal for each game is either to practice skip counting patterns or multiplication facts. We de-emphasize which team or person wins, and instead always refocus students to realize that we're all practicing together.

Crossing the River

SKILL

skip counting practice

Students enjoy getting to hop across a "river" to practice a skip counting pattern, and at the same time the students along the "shoreline" also have the opportunity to practice the skip counting movement associated with the number at hand.

Directions

1. Find an open-area in your classroom to place your "river."

2. Create the river by putting down masking tape to act as the shores of the river. Place the rubber mouse pads in the river to act as stones for students to hop across.

3. Have students line up on one bank of the river in order of age, oldest first. Beginning with the student at the front of the line, one by one, each student will roll the dice and announce the number to the group. He or she will then hop across the rocks of the river, skip-counting by the number rolled.

4. Direct the whole group to skip count with the player who is hopping and to perform the movement (for example, 7s—Alligator) while the player hops.

5. Continue playing until each player has crossed the river, or as time allows.

MATERIALS

» rubber mouse pads (up to 12)
» masking tape
» 1 pair of dice
» 1 laminated copy of the student directions, page 45 (optional)

When students are unsure of a number pattern, encourage them to look to the skip counting posters as they say the pattern. It's a good idea to teach all the students to act as checkers to be sure that the group is not practicing the wrong patterns. Checkers can also prompt another student when needed.

Supports

* When introducing this game, you may only want to use one die so students can practice skip counting by lower numbers.
* If students are not yet ready to practice all 12 numbers in a skip counting pattern, adjust the number of mouse pads accordingly.

Group It Up

This game can be a big help to those students who need to see visually how multiplication works. Students will convert number sentences into arrays. This game can also ease the transition to division for students who have difficulty grasping the concept of equal groups in multiplication and division.

SKILL

converting multiplication sentences into arrays

Directions

1. To set up, place the pile of multiplication flash cards next to a container with blocks in it.

2. Taking turns, beginning with the student closest to the classroom clock, each student selects a multiplication card from the top of the pile and says the multiplication sentence aloud.

3. Remind students that multiplication is about working with equal groups of objects. The student should then restate the problem to provide the number of groups. For example, if a student draws 3×4, he or she first states, "three times four," followed by "four groups of three."

4. The student will then arrange the blocks into an array to represent the problem they have stated.

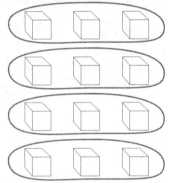

5. All students should perform the skip counting movement as they check the accuracy of the array.

6. Continue playing as time allows.

MATERIALS

» 1 stack of multiplication flash cards without products

» 1 box or bin containing 144 blocks

» 1 laminated copy of the student directions, page 46 (optional)

This game works best with groups of three or four. This enables students to get more time to practice looking at multiplication in this way.

Support

＊ Students who have difficulty with automatic fact retrieval can use skip counting to figure out the product (for example, 4, 8, 12) while touching the blocks.

Challenge

＊ Have students create a division number sentence of the array.

Concentration Multiplication

SKILL

automatic retrieval of multiplication facts

MATERIALS

» 1 laminated copy of the student directions, page 53 (optional)

💡 This is a great game to play on the bus on the way to a field trip.

O ne reason for the effectiveness of this game is that students' hands are occupied so they cannot count up on their fingers. It solidifies multiplication fact retrieval.

Directions

1. Pair up students. Practice the pattern of how this game goes in a large group before you send them off to play.

2. At the same time, each player will "slap, clap, play." Students should say "slap" while tapping their thighs, "clap" while clapping their hands, and "play" while creating a number with up to ten fingers. The numbers played by both partners become the factors in a multiplication problem.

3. Students take turns saying the entire multiplication sentence using those factors. As you circulate you should be hearing things like: "Slap, clap, play. Five times six equals thirty."

4. Challenge students to play numbers for multiplication families that are tricky to them. This is an opportunity to practice their multiplication!

5. Continue playing until time runs out.

Support

✳ If it would help your students, consider including zero as a factor. To represent zero, students should simply put out a closed fist.

Challenges

✳ Have students try this in groups of three. When they first begin with three factors, you may have each child only play with one hand out to keep factors manageable.

✳ As students gain proficiency, you may decide that certain numbers cannot be chosen (such as 1, 2, 5, 10) to help students focus on the fact families that are more challenging.

Dice Toss Relay

In this game, students have an opportunity to practice creating random completed multiplication sentences. Students each roll a set of dice and earn points for having the largest product.

Directions

1. Divide a small group into two mini teams and distribute the materials. (Each mini team should decide the order in which the team members will play.)

2. The first student on each team will toss two dice into the air (or roll on a desk) and create a multiplication sentence with the two factors rolled. For example, a student rolling a 3 and a 5 will say, "Three times five equals fifteen."

3. The team with the higher product scores a point. A team member should tally the point on the dry-erase board.

4. As each player has a turn, he or she will say a completed number sentence and record a point if appropriate.

5. When time is up, the team with the highest score wins.

Challenges

* Use 12-sided numbered dice to reinforce all of the multiplication facts.
* Have students keep track of their score mentally to practice their mental math skills.
* Change the point values given for highest and lowest product. (Start each team with 5 points. Multiply by 2 for highest product, and subtract 1 for lowest product.)
* Use fraction dice to practice addition of fractions. Students will also be able to practice comparing fractions.

SKILLS

automatic retrieval of multiplication facts

comparing whole numbers

MATERIALS

» 2 pairs of dice
» 1 dry-erase board
» 1 dry-erase marker
» 1 laminated copy of the student directions, page 48 (optional)

Blow-up dice work nicely if students will be tossing the dice in the air. Foam dice work nicely if students are going to roll the dice on a desk or table. If space is limited, students can roll the dice in a shoebox.

Multiply It

This game not only reinforces multiplication facts, but also helps students learn to pay attention and remember what their other team members have done.

Directions

1. Direct students to sit students in a circle around the dice. The player whose desk is closest to the door gets to go first.

2. Have the first player roll the two dice in the center of the circle. Using the factors rolled, he or she says a complete multiplication sentence.

3. The other students in the circle act as checkers to make sure the student says the correct product. They should give a "thumbs up" for a correct answer or say "try again" if the player needs another chance to reach the correct product.

4. As play continues in a clockwise direction, each new student must compare his or her product to that of the previous student. For example, after the student says the multiplication sentence, he or she must then say, "My product of _____ is greater/less than _____'s product of _____."

5. Continue playing until time runs out.

Support

✳ Have students write their multiplication sentences on a dry-erase board, so it's easier for them to compare the products.

Challenge

✳ Add a third die for students to practice multiplying three factors.

Operation Hop

This is a great game to help students to make smart decisions. In this game, students select number cards and then must decide which operation they are going to perform. Students only receive points if they are able to answer the math sentence correctly. However, a student can achieve a greater number of points for choosing a more difficult operation. Students hop onto the operation they are going to attempt.

SKILLS

addition

subtraction

multiplication

Directions

1. Divide a small group into two mini teams. (Each mini team should decide the order in which the team members will play.)

2. Put out the plastic bin with number cards in it. Place the operation sign mouse pads on the floor near the bin.

3. The team with the tallest player goes first.

4. The first player draws two number cards from the bin. He or she must decide whether to add, subtract, or multiply the two numbers and then hop onto the chosen sign and say the answer.
   * A correct sum earns 1 point.
   * A correct difference earns 2 points.
   * A correct product earns 4 points.
   * Incorrect answers do not earn any points.

5. Each team keeps track of their score on the dry-erase board.

6. Continue playing until time runs out. The team with the highest score wins.

MATERIALS

» 1 set of number cards (2–20)

» 1 plastic bin

» 3 operation sign mouse pads

» 1 dry-erase board

» 1 dry-erase marker

» 1 laminated copy of the student directions, page 50 (optional)

How to Make the Operation Sign Mouse Pads
• Use masking tape or a thick marker to place a large version of these operation symbols on a blank mouse pad: +, −, and ×.

Challenges

✳ Encourage students to keep track of their scores mentally, rather than on a dry-erase board.

✳ Raise the stakes by adding a buzzer. Designate a card-drawer. He or she selects two cards and shows them to the group. The first player who buzzes in and says a correct math sentence scores points for his or her team. (This should help students to see that it's not only about getting the most points, but about choosing the operation they can quickly answer.)

✳ Have students draw more than two cards to increase the complexity of their calculations. (If necessary, review with students the correct order of operations.)

Factor Toss

automatic retrieval of multiplication facts

This game is great because students' hands are occupied, so they must rely on mental skip counting or memorization in order to figure out the product. Students become competitive and simply love this game. It is a good incentive for learning their multiplication facts accurately!

MATERIALS

» soccer balls covered with numbers (1 per team)

» 1 laminated copy of the student directions, page 51 (optional)

How to Make the Numbered Soccer Balls

• Write the numbers 5–12 on every white or light-colored panel on a soccer ball using a permanent marker.

• We originally covered each face with the numbers 1–9. After students played this game a few times, we realized that it was more beneficial to have a larger selection of numbers greater than 5. We found that students did not need as much practice with the 2–5 multiplication facts.

Directions

1. First, demonstrate Factor Toss clearly with one student volunteer (because once students see the soccer balls they get very excited!). Then create teams of two or three and distribute the rest of the balls.

2. Students should hold the soccer ball so that their thumbs are close to their body.

3. Direct students to face each other and gently toss the ball to another player. (Emphasize that students should toss the ball gently. Watch out for any long passes through the classroom and consider deducting points if this occurs.)

4. When a partner catches the ball, the player looks to see where his or her thumbs landed. These become the two factors for a multiplication sentence. The player says the entire sentence aloud. For example, if the player's thumbs are on a 3 and a 6, he or she would say, "Three times six equals eighteen."

5. After receiving a thumbs up for success, the player tosses the ball back to a teammate, and the process continues as time allows.

Supports

✳ If a student's thumb lands on a line, he or she should slide it to the nearest number. Suggest picking the least or greatest number, depending on his or her level.

✳ This game can also be played as Addend Toss, in which students practice the automatic retrieval of addition facts.

Challenge

✳ Build on the Addend Toss variation with students continually adding the sums to each other. This enables students to work on mental math using larger numbers. For example, if a player's thumbs land on 8 and 7, he or she says the number sentence, "Eight plus seven equals fifteen." If the next player's thumbs land on 7 and 3, he or she says the number sentence. Then, together, the team adds the sums: "Fifteen plus ten equals twenty-five."

Multiplication Mat

With this game, students gently toss two beanbags onto a teacher-made multiplication mat. Using the numbers under the beanbags as factors, students will then say a complete multiplication sentence including the product.

Directions

1. Place the multiplication mat and beanbags on the floor.

2. Choose a starting place from which to toss the beanbags and mark it. (Consider having students stand on a square floor tile, or behind a masking tape line.)

3. The student who most recently celebrated his or her birthday goes first. He or she should stand at the starting place and throw one beanbag at a time onto the mat. The student will use the two numbers to say the complete number sentence, for example, "Four times three equals twelve."

4. Other students in the group act as checkers and give a "thumbs up" for a correct answer or say "try again" if the student needs another chance to reach the correct product.

5. After having a turn, students should retrieve the beanbags and hand them off to another player.

6. Continue playing as time allows.

Support

＊ If students need skip counting practice, use one beanbag. The number it lands on will begin the skip counting pattern and movement.

＊ Begin this game as an addition game, having students add two or three numbers together to firm up automatic addition skills.

Challenge

＊ Add a third beanbag. Have a student or a group try to multiply three factors together.

SKILL

automatic retrieval of multiplication facts

MATERIALS

» 2 beanbags
» 1 multiplication mat
» 1 laminated copy of the student directions, page 52 (optional)

How to Make the Multiplication Mat

• Glue 13 paper plates numbered 0–12 to butcher paper.

• When creating your multiplication mat, consider making it double-sided. Make one side significantly more challenging, so that this game can be played at different times throughout the school year and provide the appropriate level of challenge.

💡 You might need to put a book or basket on each corner of the mat to keep it from slipping as students toss the beanbags onto it.

Big Dice Multiplication

MATERIALS

- » 2 pairs of big dice
- » 2 empty bins
- » 1 list of shapes (circle, triangle, square, rectangle, pentagon, hexagon)
- » 1 set each of red and blue shape cards
- » 1 laminated copy of the student directions, page 47 (optional)

How to Make the Shape Cards
- Cut out the following shapes from blue and red construction paper.
  circle   rectangle
  triangle   pentagon
  square   hexagon
- Write the shape name on its shape.
- If colored construction paper isn't available, you may also draw and label each shape using a red or blue marker to create the shape card sets.
- Laminate, if desired.

💡 Large dice are a novelty that students enjoy playing with. We have also played this game using regular dice and 2-inch or 4-inch foam dice. The size of the dice mostly depends on the size of the plastic bins you have to roll them in. If you are using shoebox-sized bins, for example, the 2-inch foam dice work nicely.

This game helps the students work together as teams. It also teaches students to constantly pay attention, because otherwise they will not know whose turn will be next.

Directions

1. Divide the group into two teams, red and blue, with an equal number but no more than 6 students on a team. You'll also need to assign one extra student to be the game leader.

2. Give each student a red or blue shape card, depending on which team they are on. Be sure the same shapes are represented on both the red and blue team. Give the list of shapes to the leader.

3. Place the bins a reasonable distance away from the group (if there is room) so students get the feeling of being able to run up to the bin, which adds to the game's excitement and students' engagement. The dice should be in the bin to begin the game.

4. The leader calls out a shape from the list. The students on both teams who have that shape will move quickly to his or her team's bin.

5. Each player rolls two big dice in the bin. The numbers rolled become the factors for a complete multiplication sentence. For example, if a player rolls a 4 and a 6, he or she would say "Four times six equals twenty-four."

6. The first player to correctly say a complete, accurate multiplication sentence gains a point for his or her team.

7. Continue playing until each player has had three turns or as time allows. When we play this game, we usually tell students they are getting points, but have never actually kept track of the points. Honestly, students are just excited to get a point for their team, but don't seem to notice that no one ever wins!

Support

* If you have any students who have trouble translating the dots on dice to numbers, try using number cubes rather than traditional dice.

Challenges

* Play with 12-sided numbered dice.
* Add a third die for each bin so students can practice multiplying three factors.

Who's the Greatest?

This game helps students multiply numbers quickly and then compare products.

Directions

1. Divide a small group into two mini teams. (Each mini team should decide the order in which team members will play.)

2. Place two stacks of multiplication flash cards (1 per team) on a table or desk. Each team should line up on either side, facing each other and behind a stack of cards.

3. The first player on each team turns over a card, quickly figures out the product, and says the complete multiplication sentence.

4. Students on opposing teams then compare their products. The player who has the highest product places both teams' cards on the bottom of his or her team's stack. When the two products are equal, each team returns the card to the bottom of their stack.

5. Students take turns like a relay, moving to the back of the team line after their turn.

6. Play continues until time runs out. The team with the most cards at the end of the game wins.

Supports

* Add a dry-erase board for students to create a <, >, and = number sentence during each round.
* Play this game using only addition or subtraction flash cards.

Challenges

* Play this game using only division flash cards.
* Work on mathematics vocabulary. Ask: "Which product is larger?" or "Which sum is larger?"

SKILLS

automatic retrieval of multiplication facts

comparing products

MATERIALS

» 2 stacks of multiplication flash cards without products

» 1 laminated copy of the student directions, page 54 (optional)

The number of cards you place in a stack is flexible. Consider customizing a stack of cards to include the facts students really need to focus on.

Keep on Rollin'

Play this game to keep students' mental math skills fresh. Students first multiply two factors and then, as a team, keep a running sum of the products.

SKILLS

automatic retrieval of multiplication facts

mental addition

MATERIALS

» 2 pairs of dice-in-dice
» 2 plastic bins
» 1 laminated copy of the student directions, page 55 (optional)

Directions

1. Divide a small group into two mini teams and have them each form a line. (Each mini team should decide the order in which the team members will line up.)

2. Place one pair of dice-in-dice in each bin just out of reach of the teams.

3. The first student from each team goes up to the team's bin and rolls both dice-in-dice. First he or she must add the outside die to the inside die to get each factor. For example, if the student rolls a 3 and a 5 on one die and a 4 and 6 on the other die, the factors become 8 and 10. Then, the student must multiply the resulting factors.

4. The players announce their complete multiplication sentence. For example, "Eight times ten equals eighty."

5. Mentally, each team adds its product to the team's total score.

6. Play continues until time runs out. The team that has the highest score at the end wins.

Supports

✳ Begin this game with addition. Help students get the concepts of adding the inside and outside numbers on the dice and then keeping track of large numbers mentally.

✳ Use regular dice to work on the lower multiplication facts.

Challenge

✳ Instead of dice-in-dice, use a pair of 12-sided numbered dice.

Line Me Up

This game is great to play in the latter half of the year when students have really mastered their multiplication facts. Students quickly solve three multiplication problems and then order the products from least to greatest.

SKILLS

automatic retrieval of multiplication facts

comparing whole numbers

Directions

1. Provide a stack of multiplication flash cards.

2. Each student in a small group should draw a card and solve the multiplication problem mentally.

3. Students will then line up so their products are in ascending order.

4. Beginning with the lowest product, have each player say his or her complete multiplication sentence.

5. If necessary, have group members adjust the line so they are in the order of the least to greatest product.

6. Continue playing as time allows.

MATERIALS

» 1 stack of multiplication flash cards without products

» 1 laminated copy of the student directions, page 56 (optional)

Supports

✻ Assign different roles to the students. For example, assign one student to be the fact checker and another to be the group captain. The fact checker checks each product to make sure it is correct before the captain lines up the students so their products go in ascending order.

✻ Give students a dry-erase board. Have them write a math sentence using the <, >, and = signs to show how their products compare.

Challenges

✻ This game provides an opportunity for you to teach students the order of operations using parentheses. Have students take their multiplication problems and write them out horizontally on a dry-erase board. Then, have students add their products together and think about whether order matters when writing out these problems. Have students create <, >, and = sentences using the original problems with parentheses.

✻ Have students each take three multiplication problems, solve them, and then compare the products without their team's help.

Pick a Product

This game allows students to look at multiplication in a different way and to grasp division concepts.

SKILLS

finding all possible factors

divisibility rules

MATERIALS

» 1 stack of product cards

» dry-erase boards (1 per team)

» dry-erase markers (1 per team)

» 1 laminated copy of the student directions, page 57 (optional)

How to Make the Product Cards

• Number a stack of index cards with the products 2–25. The product should appear larger, in the middle of the card.

• In the top right corner of the card, write a small number that indicates how many ways there are to get the product. Use the following chart for reference:

How Many Ways	Product
2	2, 3, 5, 7, 11, 13, 17, 19, 23
3	4, 9, 25
4	6, 8, 10, 14, 15, 21, 22
5	16
6	12, 18, 20
8	24

Add various product cards to the stack or remove others to suit the level of your students.

• Laminate, if desired.

Directions

1. Divide students into teams. Direct these student teams to sit in their own circle around a stack of product cards that are facedown in the center. Each team should choose a card turner and a score recorder.

2. Distribute a dry-erase board and marker to each team.

3. Select one student on each team to turn over the product card and read the number aloud. As team members determine the number of ways to get to the product, the team's recorder should write the answers on the dry-erase board.

4. Every time a team can identify all the ways to get the product (as noted in the card's upper right corner), the team scores a point.

5. Play continues as time allows. The team with the most points wins.

Supports

✳ Provide students with manipulatives to use. For example, students can count out the number of cubes for a product and then try different group sizes to see if the product is divisible by different numbers. Show students how to use trial-and-error to discover all of the ways to get the product.

✳ Provide students with array charts and have them create arrays for the product. (If you laminate an array chart, students can use it repeatedly with an overhead marker.)

Mystery Number

In this game, students create clues to describe a "mystery number." The other team members try to guess the correct answer.

Directions

1. Divide students into teams with 3–5 players each. Students work as teams to determine what the mystery number is based on clues.

2. Distribute a stack of Mystery Number cards to each team. Tell students that the player on each team who has the most letters in his or her last name goes first. (Play then continues in a clockwise direction.)

3. One at a time, each student will draw a mystery number from the pile and come up with three clues for his or her team members. (Possible hints include whether the number is odd or even, prime or composite, and so on. Students might also say, "One of its factors is ___," or "It's a multiple of ___.")

4. The other students on the team take turns guessing what number it could be. When a student suggests the wrong number, the clue giver explains which clue or clues the number does not fit.

5. After five incorrect guesses, the player should add another clue to help guide his or her teammates' guesses to the right answer. However, once these further clues are given, the team forfeits the ability to earn a point for that turn.

6. Continue playing as time allows. The team with the most points wins.

Support

✳ Create a hint sheet for the type of clues students might ask. For example:
  • My number is odd/even. (Students could circle one.)
  • If you added ___ to my number it would equal _____.
The types of clues that students use should be based on concepts already taught in the school year.

SKILL

number sense

MATERIALS

» 1 stack of Mystery Number cards
» 1 laminated copy of the student directions, page 58 (optional)

How to Make the Mystery Number Cards
• Number a stack of index cards with the following numbers:

2	17	26
3	18	27
4	19	30
5	21	31
9	23	35
10	24	36
12	25	

We recommend these numbers because they include a variety of qualities—odd/even, prime/composite, and so on. Feel free to use any numbers that best fit your students' needs.

• Decorate the other side of the cards with a question mark or simply leave blank.

• Laminate, if desired.

First to 50

In this game, students use mathematical reasoning to decide how to use the numbers they roll on dice so they eventually equal exactly fifty. Students will have to add, subtract, multiply, and divide—and keep track carefully along the way—to make it all work out!

Directions

1. Form teams of 3–4 students.

2. Distribute dice to each team.

3. Tell students that the goal for this game is to be the first team to get exactly 50 points.

4. The student sitting closest to the clock goes first. He or she will roll the two dice. That player will decide to add, subtract, multiply, or divide the two numbers he or she has rolled. (The answer must always be a positive whole number.)

5. Going clockwise, all subsequent players will roll the two dice deciding what operation to use for the two numbers rolled.

6. At the end of each turn, the team must decide how to apply that number to the total score so far (by adding, subtracting, multiplying, or dividing). If students choose to divide, they may not use remainders.

7. Continue playing until a team has exactly 50 points.

Support

* Try this game first with just addition and subtraction so students can get used to how it works.
* Have students extend the 2s skip counting pattern to 50.

Challenges

* Make the target score lower to increase the game difficulty.
* Change the game so the students receive different point values depending on which operation they use. You can control which operations you want the students to focus on this way.

Super-Fun Multiplication Memory Boosters © 2013 by Kathleen Kelly and Stephanie Nunziata, Scholastic Teaching Resources

Karate Chops

3

6

9

12

15

18

21

24

27

30

33

36

Windshield Wipers

2

4

6

8

10

12

14

16

18

20

22

24

Baseball Throws

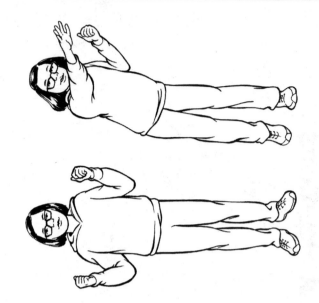

5
10
15
20
25
30
35
40
45
50
55
60

Head Taps

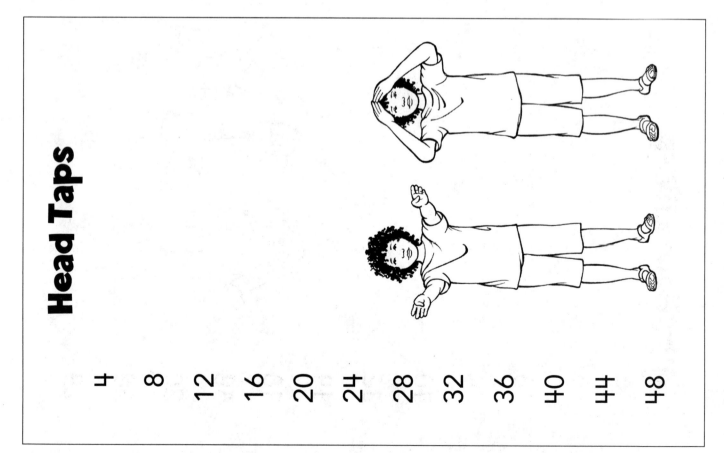

4
8
12
16
20
24
28
32
36
40
44
48

Alligators

7
14
21
28
35
42
49
56
63
70
77
84

Heel Lifts

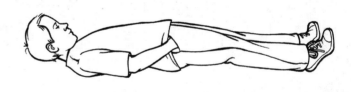

6
12
18
24
30
36
42
48
54
60
66
72

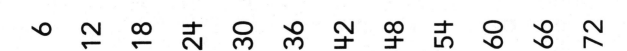

Knee Lifts

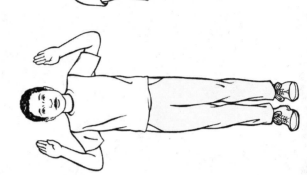

9

18

27

36

45

54

63

72

81

90

99

108

Star Pulls

8

16

24

32

40

48

56

64

72

80

88

96

Lap Claps

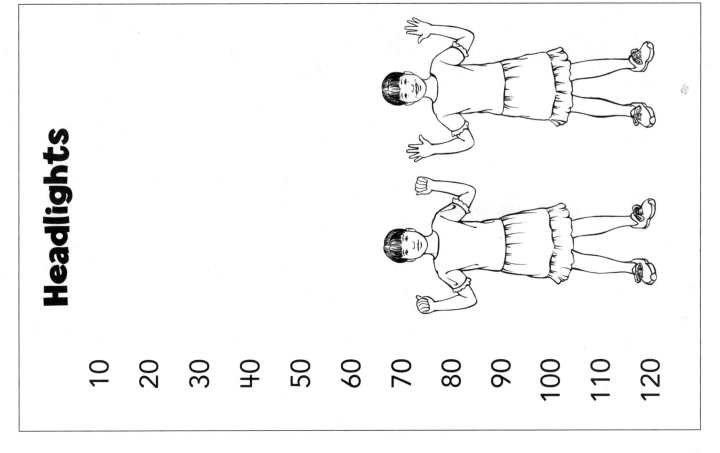

11

22

33

44

55

66

77

88

99

110

121

132

Headlights

10

20

30

40

50

60

70

80

90

100

110

120

Shoulder Shrugs

12

24

36

48

60

72

84

96

108

120

132

144

Name: _____ Date: _____

Hundred Block

Follow your teacher's directions to work with the Hundred Block.

1	2	3	4	5	6	7	8	9	10
11	12	13	14	15	16	17	18	19	20
21	22	23	24	25	26	27	28	29	30
31	32	33	34	35	36	37	38	39	40
41	42	43	44	45	46	47	48	49	50
51	52	53	54	55	56	57	58	59	60
61	62	63	64	65	66	67	68	69	70
71	72	73	74	75	76	77	78	79	80
81	82	83	84	85	86	87	88	89	90
91	92	93	94	95	96	97	98	99	100

Name: _____

Date: _____

Number Chain

Start each chain with a number (2–12), then complete the chain by writing the numbers in that skip-counting pattern (example: 3 . . . 6, 9, 12, 15, 18, 21, 24, 27, 30, 33, 36).

Crossing the River

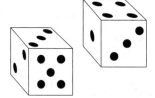

DIRECTIONS

1 Line up along the one bank of the river in order of age, oldest first.

2 Beginning with the student at the front of the line, one by one, each player will roll the dice. Tell your group the number you have rolled.

3 Use this number to begin your journey across the river. As you move from one stone to the next, say the skip counting pattern for the number you rolled.

4 The players along the shore skip count with the river-crosser.

5 Continuing down the line, the other players cross the river in the same way.

Group It Up

**3
×12**

DIRECTIONS

1 Whoever is closest to the classroom clock goes first! Select a multiplication problem off the top of the pile.

2 Say the multiplication sentence aloud.

3 Multiplication is about working with equal groups of objects. Turn your multiplication sentence around, by taking the numbers of the card you drew and saying them differently. For example, say, "three times four is four groups of three."

4 Use the blocks to create a picture of the number sentence you're working with. This type of multiplication picture is called an array.

5 Once you've built the array, teammates should check your work. Then, they will give a "thumbs up" or say "try again." (Be sure to clean up for the next player.)

6 Take turns repeating the steps until each player has selected five multiplication problems, or until time is up.

Super-Fun Multiplication Memory Boosters © 2013 by Kathleen Kelly and Stephanie Nunziata, Scholastic Teaching Resources

Concentration Multiplication

DIRECTIONS

1 With a partner, practice the "slap, clap, play" motions of this game. Say,
* "slap" while tapping your thighs.
* "clap" while clapping your hands.
* "play" while putting out a number with your fingers (up to ten).

The number you create with your fingers will become a factor. Your partner's number will become the other factor.

2 Take turns saying a complete multiplication sentence that includes the two factors and a product.

3 This is a time for practicing multiplication facts. Challenge yourself to put out factors that are tricky!

4 Continue playing until time is up.

Dice Toss Relay

DIRECTIONS

1 Decide in what order your team will play.

2 One player at a time, toss your team's dice. Create a complete multiplication sentence using the numbers you tossed as the factors.

3 Say your multiplication sentence aloud. For example, if you roll a 3 and a 5, your multiplication sentence is 3 × 5 = 15. You would say, "Three times five equals fifteen."

4 The team that has the higher product scores 2 points. The team with the lower product scores 1 point.

5 Keep track of your team's score. When time is up, the team with the highest score wins.

 Super-Fun Multiplication Memory Boosters © 2013 by Kathleen Kelly and Stephanie Nunziata, Scholastic Teaching Resources

Multiply It

DIRECTIONS

1 Your group should be sitting in a circle. The player whose desk is closest to the door goes first.

2 Roll the dice in the center of the circle.

3 Using the factors rolled, say a complete multiplication sentence.

4 The rest of the group checks the math. Give a "thumbs up" for a correct answer. Say, "Try again," if the player needs another chance to reach the correct product.

5 As play continues in a clockwise direction, compare your product to the student who went before you. Say, "My product of ____ is greater than (or less than) _____'s product of ____."

6 Continue playing until time is up.

Operation Hop

DIRECTIONS

1 One player from your team
goes up to the bin and selects two number cards.

2 The player must decide whether he or she can
accurately add, subtract, or multiply the two numbers,
and hop onto that operation sign.

3 The player then says the complete number sentence.
If he or she correctly
* adds the numbers, the team receives 1 point.
* subtracts the numbers, the team receives 2 points.
* multiplies the numbers, the team receives 4 points.

Incorrect answers do not receive any points.

4 Keep track of your team's score. When time is up, the
team with the highest score wins.

Factor Toss

DIRECTIONS

1 Hold the ball so that your thumbs are close to your body and face your partner.

2 Gently toss the ball to your partner.

3 When you catch the ball, look where your thumbs landed. These two numbers become the factors in your multiplication sentence. (If your thumbs land on a line, shift your thumb to the closest number.)

4 Say the complete multiplication sentence with the product. The waiting partner should check your thinking and give a thumbs up when you've said a correct product.

5 When you've gotten the thumbs up, toss the ball gently back to your partner (or another team member) for his or her turn.

6 Continue playing until time is up.

Multiplication Mat

DIRECTIONS

1 The student who most recently celebrated his or her birthday goes first. On your turn, stand at the starting place.

2 Toss one beanbag at a time onto the Multiplication Mat.

3 Create a multiplication sentence using the two numbers your beanbags landed on. Say the complete sentence aloud. For example, if you land on a 4 and a 3, say "Four times three equals twelve."

4 The rest of the group will help check the answer. They should give a "thumbs up" if it is a correct product, or say, "try again," if the player needs to think about his or her answer one more time.

5 After completing a turn, the player should hand off the beanbags to the next player to take a turn.

6 Continue playing until time is up.

Big Dice Multiplication

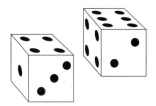

DIRECTIONS

1 Your teacher will divide you into two teams: red and blue. The teacher will also give each player a shape card and assign a leader.

2 When the team leader calls the shape of the card in your hand, quickly move to your team's bin. Roll both dice. These numbers become the factors in your multiplication sentence.

3 Say the complete multiplication sentence. For example, if you roll a 4 and a 6, your multiplication sentence is 4 × 6 = 24. You would say, "Four times six equals twenty-four."

4 The first player to give an accurate multiplication sentence earns a point for his or her team.

5 Continue playing until each player has had three turns or until time is up.

Who's the Greatest?

$$\begin{array}{r} 12 \\ \times\ 3 \\ \hline \end{array}$$

DIRECTIONS

1 Each team lines up behind a stack of cards. Teams should be facing each other.

2 The first player in each line flips over a card. He or she solves the problem and says the complete multiplication sentence aloud.

3 The two players compare their two products. The player with the greater product receives both cards and puts both cards at the bottom of the team's pile. If a tie occurs, teams keep their own multiplication card and place it on the bottom of their pile.

4 Once a player has had a turn, he or she should move to the back of the line.

5 Play continues until time is up.

Keep on Rollin'

DIRECTIONS

1 The first player from each team will go up to its bin and roll one die. Add the inside and outside number from the die.

2 Roll the other die. Add the inside and outside number from that die.

3 Use the two numbers as factors and multiply them.

4 Tell everyone the complete multiplication sentence.

5 Using mental math, each team adds the product to their score.

6 Continue playing until time is up. The team with the highest total score at the end of the game wins!

Line Me Up

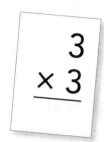

DIRECTIONS

1 Each player selects a card.

2 Solve the multiplication problem in your head.

3 Line up so your products go from least to greatest. (The group member with the lowest product should be at one end of the line. The one with the greatest product should be at the other end of the line.)

4 Each player should say his or her complete multiplication sentence. All players should listen to figure out if the group is in the correct order.

5 If necessary, line up your group again so the products go in order from least to greatest, then share your results with another group.

6 Continue playing until time is up.

Pick a Product

DIRECTIONS

1 Sit with your team in a circle, around a pile of product cards.

2 Select a team card turner and a team score recorder.

3 The card turner turns over one product card. The large number in the center of the card is the product, and the small number in upper right corner is the number of ways to get the product.

4 The team will try to figure out all the different way to get the product on the card you pick.

5 The team recorder writes the different ways on the dry-erase board. Every time your team can identify the same number of ways as the number in the upper right corner, you get a point.

6 Continue playing until time is up.

Mystery Number

DIRECTIONS

1 The player who is facing the window goes first. Play will continue in a clockwise direction.

2 The first player selects a Mystery Number Card and looks at it secretly. The player must come up with three clues to describe the Mystery Number. Here are some ideas to use:

* The Mystery Number is _____ (odd or even).
* The Mystery Number is a _____ (prime or composite) number.
* The Mystery Number is a factor of _____.
* One of the Mystery Number's factors is _____.

Be creative with your clues. If you can think of other ways to describe your mystery number, then go for it!

3 If the team guesses incorrectly, guide the team toward what clue they might be overlooking, or the one that does not work for their guess.

4 After five wrong guesses, provide the team with another clue. If this is necessary, you cannot earn a point.

5 Continue playing until time is up. The team with the most points wins.

 Super-Fun Multiplication Memory Boosters © 2013 by Kathleen Kelly and Stephanie Nunziata, Scholastic Teaching Resources

First to 50

DIRECTIONS

1 The player who is sitting closest to the clock goes first. Play continues in a clockwise direction.

2 The first player rolls the dice. He or she decides whether to add, subtract, multiply, or divide the two numbers rolled. This becomes the first score.

3 The second player rolls the dice. He or she decides whether to add, subtract, multiply, or divide those numbers. (The resulting number must be a whole number that is greater than zero.)

4 The team then decides how to take that new number and apply it to the score. The team may add, subtract, multiply, or divide it by their score. (Again, the resulting number must be a positive whole number greater than zero.)

5 The first team to have a total of exactly 50 points wins.

Name: _____   Date: _____

Skip Counting Assessment

Fill in as many missing numbers as you can.

7, 14, ____, ____, ____, ____, 49, ____, ____, ____, ____, ____

____, ____, ____, 8, 10, 12, ____, ____, ____, 20, ____, ____

12, 24, 36, ____, 60, ____, ____, 96, ____, ____, ____, ____

11, ____, 33, ____, 55, ____, ____, ____, ____, 110, ____, ____

____, 10, 15, ____, ____, ____, ____, 40, ____, ____, ____, ____

10, ____, ____, ____, ____, 60, ____, ____, ____, ____, ____, 120

9, 18, ____, ____, 45, ____, ____, 72, ____, ____, ____, ____

3, 6, 9, ____, ____, ____, ____, ____, 27, ____, ____, ____

____, ____, 24, 32, 40, ____, ____, ____, ____, 80, ____, ____

6, 12, ____, ____, ____, ____, 42, ____, ____, ____, ____, ____

____, 8, 12, ____, ____, ____, ____, 32, ____, ____, ____, ____

Name: _____   Date: _____

Multiplication Assessment

Finish as many multiplication problems as you can.

$7 \times 9 =$ ___	$6 \times 4 =$ ___	$3 \times 5 =$ ___	$9 \times 9 =$ ___	$8 \times 7 =$ ___
$\begin{array}{r} 3 \\ \times\ 4 \\ \hline \end{array}$	$\begin{array}{r} 8 \\ \times\ 3 \\ \hline \end{array}$	$\begin{array}{r} 5 \\ \times\ 8 \\ \hline \end{array}$	$\begin{array}{r} 9 \\ \times\ 6 \\ \hline \end{array}$	$\begin{array}{r} 7 \\ \times\ 2 \\ \hline \end{array}$
$3 \times 4 =$ ___	$4 \times 8 =$ ___	$11 \times 5 =$ ___	$12 \times 12 =$ ___	$10 \times 6 =$ ___
$\begin{array}{r} 10 \\ \times\ 11 \\ \hline \end{array}$	$\begin{array}{r} 12 \\ \times\ 8 \\ \hline \end{array}$	$\begin{array}{r} 7 \\ \times\ 6 \\ \hline \end{array}$	$\begin{array}{r} 3 \\ \times\ 9 \\ \hline \end{array}$	$\begin{array}{r} 2 \\ \times\ 9 \\ \hline \end{array}$
$4 \times 4 =$ ___	$11 \times 7 =$ ___	$9 \times 4 =$ ___	$2 \times 8 =$ ___	$5 \times 4 =$ ___
$\begin{array}{r} 3 \\ \times\ 7 \\ \hline \end{array}$	$\begin{array}{r} 7 \\ \times\ 5 \\ \hline \end{array}$	$\begin{array}{r} 6 \\ \times\ 6 \\ \hline \end{array}$	$\begin{array}{r} 5 \\ \times\ 5 \\ \hline \end{array}$	$\begin{array}{r} 3 \\ \times\ 10 \\ \hline \end{array}$
$11 \times 10 =$ ___	$2 \times 12 =$ ___	$8 \times 9 =$ ___	$2 \times 3 =$ ___	$4 \times 8 =$ ___

Dear Parents,

The school-home connection is an important one for our children. Schools work best when we all work together on behalf of our learners. As we teach your child math facts, we want to offer you some strategies to help along the way. Below is a collection of activities that you can do with your child to help reinforce his or her recall of math facts. This reinforcement makes it easier for students to retrieve these facts quickly and accurately when needed. This is an absolutely essential ability in higher level math activities, when the focus needs to be on thinking, not on computing!

Addition/Subtraction Activities

Always have addition/subtraction fact flash cards with you when you are on the go (punch holes and place them on a ring to keep them together). Have your child say the problems out loud and tell you the answers.

While walking down the street, for example, find two numbers in the immediate environment (license plates, address numbers, street numbers, and so on) to make an addition or subtraction problem . . . then ask your child to solve it!

Skip Counting

While waiting at a red light, for example, have your child practice skip counting until the light turns green. Want to make it more interesting? Encourage your child pick a number from the license plate of the car in front of you to start skip counting!

As you go down an aisle at the supermarket, use the number of the aisle to start the skip counting. Have your child say the next number in the series each time you add an item to the cart in that aisle (on aisle #4, he or she will say "four, eight, twelve, sixteen . . .").

Multiplication Activities

Always have multiplication fact flash cards with you when you are on the go (again, punch holes and place them on a ring). Have your child say the problems out loud and tell you the answers.

At the dinner table, have your child roll two dice before dessert (do it five times!). He or she can say the multiplication problems and then the answers!

Play "I'm thinking of a number . . ." anytime. Tell your child you're thinking of a number and give specific information about the number (such as, "I'm thinking of a number that is equal to five times three"). Let your child answer five of these before you move on to another activity.

Sincerely,

Super-Fun Multiplication Memory Boosters © 2013 by Kathleen Kelly and Stephanie Nunziata, Scholastic Teaching Resources

Dear Parents,

As we move into the latter part of our school year, we would like to take this opportunity to touch base with you regarding your child's mathematical development. As we know, the study of mathematics is a sequential endeavor, in which the first steps are crucially important for development of a firm foundational understanding of numbers and arithmetic. We are committed to helping your child become the most capable mathematician he or she can be. To that end, we have been working all year to develop multiple pathways for their math learning, including: teacher modeling, extensive practice, kinesthetic, or tactile/physical learning activities, and memory-link development using "math moves."

At this point, we would like to clarify some teaching goals we have so you will be better able to support your child's math learning at home. Together, we can help your child find great success in future math endeavors.

By midyear, your child should . . .

• know the basic addition and subtraction facts up to 12.

• have earned a certificate in the classroom for knowing the basic math facts.

• be familiar with skip-counting using the numbers 2 through 12
  (up to the first 10 numbers in each series).

By the end of the school year, your child should . . .

• demonstrate confidence in the basic addition and subtraction facts
  up to 20.

• demonstrate a basic knowledge of the multiplication facts up to 6s.

We know that your child's success is as important to you as it is to us. We look forward to seeing your child benefit from our efforts at school in combination with your efforts at home so that he or she can become a confident math learner ready for third grade!

Sincerely,

I learned my math facts!

_____
Student

has learned the math facts

for the number(s) _____.

That's really great!

_____
Date

_____
Teacher